# CLUTCHING LAMBS

# CLUTCHING LAMBS

## Janet Passehl

A Negative Capability Press Book

Published in the United States of America by
Negative Capability Press
Mobile, Alabama

Text Copyright © by Janet Passehl
ISBN # — 978-0-942544-28-2
Library of Congress Control Number:  2015937325

Production and design by Christopher Passehl Graphic Design

Printed in the United States of America

Cover and inside photographs by Christopher Passehl.
Figurine by A. Pepe, Naples, Italy

Visit Negative Capability Press
at
negativecapabiitypress.org
facebook.com/negativecapabilitypress

*for Chris,*
*my lion-hearted*

CLUTCHING LAMBS

Liquescence

While everything else is solid and grieving

**body: any bounded aggregate of matter.**

**(C)love(n)**

Liquescence

**Egress**

Three will be in the house

                will not be eglantine

                      fine and rooms

    in the mind

Three will not be home before

                     the long plait of hills


Quarternion three women plus baby's

           thigh

        blue bronze scarlet shrewd


Curlew

            following cloak-ward listening


These will not be in the house

                  of an evening paling:

      a garment ending *een*

          shiftless hollow behind the knee

            *

One third tendon one third hapless one third sated

Across tar wild grass saplings

To the top of water small unblue

Green is yellow there

The rest is texture instantaneous

Hissing silken watery

Where the baby with fat under his skin, fat to accommodate

Growth where larden buoyant

He floats atop

His will not be in the house tonight:  warm brittle dry


*


Harm will be warm in the house

will be urgent pine chest

carriage

Three will be alone before

his strange footprint

Waiting bird a light blinking small continent wallow

## and scant to make your bed


No one hears you thinking.

The call came yesterday and you sank beneath cushions.
It hit you hard, the grape that is a rock.
Perfect in your palm and weighty as belligerence.

With no one to help you quell the fibers, loneliness breaks out of its seed
        and makes baby chick noises. Sorry

        doesn't fathom your depths.

        Settled now, the man wets his mouth.
            *Enough smothers destiny.*

If the bird were blue, like its egg, it would be invisible against the sky on a bright day.
She must have a mate, my pear tree, as she has borne one pear yearly, heavy and juicy.

Need carries the brook beside its banks, to the shore, in the wet as alteration
always recognizable though, as water.

        *The scene shifts to God.*

        Dogskin, make-up and water-pulped vegetables.
        Words come out of a machine, come voiceless.

It is no God.
*No god whatever.*
*Here.*
        *In heaven.*

Below, the severed grass
and cage and wants.

**Friction**


Caressed by emptiness, it rubs you.

You rock on the old hassock month after
month and the drama laughs back.

Four improper limbs fold into the Spitfire.
No reverse. This is your going.

Choke and finger
the ash in your pocket until you spill it
on the gritty mat.

If the world is a horse what does it matter

that you were once an engine.

**Gate That Hunger Opened**

feastless dream

no food, machine

nor science of the holy

that you might chew on souls

or on those that are only soul

and grow by the grace of sun

once eaten are soil, or weaken or

vapor

enough is not without the palace walls

the place of spoken

walls nor much beheld or heard

by souls dining

on boulders

climb and sup and hide behind

what might have been divine

or equal, that evening fell a leveling

of sun and earth

## A Holy Day

In all your actions do you wish to be praised like a child or deceive or make an impression or eat a fig? An action like eating a fig: cover it over with all your mouth. Inside your eye where there is no space. But there is a room where the floor is curved and you roll around on it and think you are as smart as a pig.

A little pig born in March. The pig is secretly killed and roasted in an oven.

Today is a special time. Good follows like dust behind a camel and your red tongue tastes like cherry sugar, in other words, childish. The couch is a bore. There is no such thing as original sin but all obstacles are a virtue. Have I mentioned the epiphany of your languid legs, stretched out straight, and bare?

**Them**

We ate and slept under the long sky.

We were nothing, and our nothingness pierced me
pinning me to this unknown place.
They kept asking for water.

I found water and kept it a secret
to wash away my smell and clean
the tangled mane that used to be my mantle.

One by one they baked into impenetrable hardness
and when they died I washed them
and left them to boil back to supple flesh
so they could rot.

Saturated, darkening limbs claw the white sky

Between each rock stretches an envelope of the dying

How swell you look today, the wetlands flooding

Your estuarial heart

Deer, I invite you to my party

On the big water stain on the road

Come after dark

Come to the stain in the shape of Alaska

Dragging your leg

I'll be there with flashlight and boots

**Shed them**

Two gray animals climbed the stairs

      but I held to my mother

            I swayed with my mother

      In my little mind

            I danced on a penny

Their coats grew

      cold on the porch

      Their coats shed

            warmth as they were

      shed

I hungered hard like a plastic toy

      without appetite

            I salivated

      and slaked at a breast

I vibrated with the hum of tvs and heaters

      while those without power

            shuddered

            between dogs

      in a field across town

            where a baby could freeze

## Love, Ice-blind

I cannot count the rails for dark has fallen.

This night has lasted weeks, my shrew, my wolf.

What waits across the tundra? Run with me.

Leap the ridges where the ice has broken

time into a blind, wracked abyss

The fever of your temper blots the cold.

Your howl melts the stiff unsounding bliss

of emptiness.

Now I am still and moving,

on a train for I have left you

frozen, there.

The ground beneath me passes like a squall–

furious, stealthless, rigid, biting, gone.

I peer out at the lights because their blaze

reminds me of your snow-encrusted hair.

**after *Død Hund***

*(a painting by Bjørn Carlsen in the Astrup Fearnley Museum, Oslo)*

If only we would be stolid,
the living and the dead,
the painted hound,
downed fleeting,
earless, red-eyed, wild-
footed ghost, museum-bound,
her fur in a lock-
et on a chain
around my neck.

My therapist says griefs ride each others' coat-tails; my swift white dog
        a jet-stream of losses: mother, brother, swimming children shot in their backs.

I need the vaunted ceiling
to which the dead rise,
stroke by stroke behind
a door where one cut rose
browns, planted in the bronze
fist of a crying saint.

I ride the bus to see the fleet ships grounded
on their mounts,
once mounds
beneath which human
beings mortified.

I buy shoes and carry them all night,
to the gallery, to the opera, to an iceberg, and return
to find you coughing in front of a tv show about plane crashes.
I lie down beside you on the bed.

I uncover at the gate each house

invite the young husband (to stay) who is old and

unsaid

carry forth the ruins, this time shoving hundreds of minutes

      broken out into years

      like bombs

      I stayed,

      after the catastrophe

to field investigations, my own, my skin,

into ska, warm beer and hips

tongues whirred into the consonance of night

swallowed morning

      knocked back the glottal day, each and its next

      tramped over streets that led

      to a place where my back turned back against my chest

and the narrow space left to myself

who am old and in some way remain

unwed

**Skyscraping Snow White**

Doc throws down pills from the balcony above.

They land softly in the plush of your palm like baby teeth

waiting to be sown back into your mouth.

Rain pings on the hard snow, the snow changes.

Deep song ruptures a frozen crust, absorbs the thin music that has befallen us.

I grab the railing of this ellipsis in time.

For now

you may:

eat a sweet apple and sing,

strum your guitar with a thumb grafted onto the bud

of tomorrow . . .

A wilted amaranth, still red though flaked and rimmed with brown,

rough-woven blanket hanging down to dry and chill, and you

erect on a terrace while the building shimmies around you, your legs

identical as gravestones

planted in the concrete sky,

the window an arch-

ed, etched mirror throwing back

good luck.

Imagine, I wake you.

**A place she can't go**

She would have waited for him but there she was, standing at the door where she stands. The effort to put things where they belong is too much. She can barely hear him when he looks at her.

It is just too much to be left alone like this, he thinks. A buzzer will bring a nurse, clean water. Soap and towels quell the desertion a little bit, but bring fresh distress to the question that rests on the windowsill. What wilting is such sorrow to the hope of those newly ones.

A tube is a shape of space between two places: a one-way passage.

His aspiration is weak, she says. She shifts bluely inside her gown, thinking she wants to be the sky. So he can be the air-plane that flies through her.

In a room below, people murmur as they view a deep wound. They change locations around a table.

**The giving boundary**

white sails immaculately

      nascent above reflection he

            cocks a finger into the filamental layer

      between surface

            and submersion


      stings what is otherwise soft and agile as a kiss

gleaming and silking as mica she comes, he frog-

      leaps breaking obsidian

            mirror open before him

      for him

            a mouth

                  whose tongue he rides out

      his body's reefs

            and clefts

**Dear rowboat,**


This depression is where the man drowned the day his dog wandered home.

Dear rowboat, the flag shimmies in the foreground, shrouds around its pole. Sarah will buy this place when she wins the lottery, if I don't. You are not the ghost ship, hardly, the one we watched last night, drifting. I'm so sorry about Don, but anyway I put lipstick on this morning like always. Simply said, there's no substitute for a well-defined pair of lips.

The *chhht chhht* of Sarah's broom on the boards sounds like "cheat cheat," but this I will never do. Not as long as the horizon stays well away out there where some god placed it. "Despair despair" mimics no activity I can name. There is no time so quiet as high tide. Bodies are gone, heads glide and sip the silver-blue. I meant, dear rowboat, to write about a river, but now I fear this is the ocean.

**Master Builder**

IV.

Mine, in a minimal human presence, survives. Wastewater rings living things and buildings are mistaken as writing. By the clumped ancient yews that cluster at the little church, a dark smudge is indicated. A number reminds us where a preacher stands, and smaller figures in priestly garb set amid these discreet physical features imagine the reverse. Which walls have been held up? These dry walls indicate a larger presence that masks the disinhabiting. In part, these are where the preacher stands when he is unraveling the great gable that represents the church. Dwellings might imagine that they grew that way as a natural feature establishes strata. But in fact architecture is indicated.

I am beginning my picture today, whoever dares to answer.   If only the boy
      were in the drawing.

White light gives up its colors in an enclosure where a boy lies

            back on a bed

                        his room a deep narrow pool with him at the bottom

            floating on a white cotton mattress

                  with softly rounded corners and a wrinkle.

        Fog obscures his reading and he is blurred by a movement
              from the book to his dark
                        head behind the book from the pages flipping faster
                  than he can run. The pages spitting out letters
                              There is no such thing as white. I have forgotten it.

                                    The boy at the edge

      of the lens is unfocused. His room is the width of one

                  mattress and he holds a gloss-
            covered book above his face with a small hand
      tinted by a chosen strand of blue
                  light. His spine rounds, a taut bow ready to send its arrow

            into the text.

                              *

There is only one man who passes
quickly seen from inside through the greenish flare of
                            the dark spots that might be the tops of leafy trees
the window unseen by the boy
because the book holds the boy
                    or the spaces
                            between stars at night


                    *



Curled up like a turtle on its back, feet against the paned
                    glass: is he drowning or skating?
                                    Boy

His room backs up
                    to a gray parking lot and a building with railed
                    porches. A van. Everything silver except the boy and alizarin
                    crimson envelopes from his imagination.
                                    A tree

    is the architect's dream. Like a child's drawing rooms
                            are stacked two on two and numbered one
                    through four. Plants on the floor, everything on the floor
                            with soft depressions from high heeled shoes
                        blankets, a hundredth of a second, a musical clock

There is room for a leaning bicycle and the only colors that ever
        glow are blue, red and a slight green.

    The alleyway between the houses blurs and you step through
a contagion.

    Violent angles like nunchucks

                            in blankets, a hundredth of a second, a musical clock
No shoes are to be seen, only folded
        blouses
            blankets, a hundredth of a second, a musical clock

        and one rectangle of paper with an angled crease.

## The Architect's Sleep Is
## Flat and Deep

Stranded branches deft
pencil strokes the man
who is kneeling knows
he is on the other side
of the glass and
bending toward a glass
of water on the floor
he is muted by frosted
glass and nowhere near
the side street where a
woman in a white coat
walks away

Power lines drawn and
splayed in a sky uniform
blue except as light is cast
on the hull of its ovoid
shape
the sky lit
by square white houses
houses those stars
by which time is told hold
and brace
the fluid envelope

Windows align in perilous
telescopic squares front to
back as if there would be
no drama between them
in      fact      emptiness
magnetizes   space   and
elsewhere tines of a chair
and spined
things indiscernible from
this  distance  split  the
oblong                absence

**The house is as clear as the panes in their steel frames**

One room is for eating, sleeping, singing, sex and accounting.

There is a desk, a music stand, a thin brown mattress and a white rug across which to navigate spillage and regret.

A child, bowl and fork.

Yellow dishes, hair-dye, old newspapers and crayon drawings of the moon.

A sinuous pot-bound tree mimics the form of antlers on a young buck, pregnant red tips so tender this is no room for a human.

**September 13, 2008**

Dear Kazuko,
the thing is to work
with gravity
rather than defy it.
Grow the house
up plant-like
from a center
stalk. The earth
is round and so
must the house
be, a helmet
for the psyche
of our daily lives,
although R. Buckminster Fuller
wasn't much interested
in the psyche,
except as it tricks us
into complacencies
such as insisting the sun
rises in the morning
though we know it doesn't.
I stopped by your gallery
on Rivington Street today.
The door was locked
but your step-ladder
was standing there, as if
you'd just descended,
your pit-bull puppy lying
behind the glass
door in a parallelogram
of sun-light,
blond and tender
as a sleeping baby. I hadn't planned
to be on the Lower East Side
but it was Chris's birthday
and he wanted to trade

the electric for an acoustic
at Rivington Guitar. The house
begins with a bombing, a violent
hole in the ground
in which home is planted
like a seed. The actual
structure is delivered
via rocket. The house
can withstand thousand-
mile-an-hour winds
because it folds
and gives,
instead of resisting. Perhaps
it wasn't meant to be
a helmet at all, but a shower-cap
or the cranium
of a newborn. I knocked
and knocked
and waited and walked
up and down the block
smelling sugar
and salsa and raw
fish, looking for you
but you weren't anywhere.
So we went to the Whitney
to see the R. Buckminster
Fuller show. Kazuko,
your buttery infant
dog Shintaro
rolled onto his back,
presenting his pink
belly and tiny penis
to the old immigrant women
who looked through the glass
and laughed.

**Breath is a distance**

> that cannot be breached

by sermon

> how the prow of a ship breaks ice    is how language moves

when circularity

> ruptures    vocabulary

sunders   meaning

becomes a direction only a sigh can travel because

> endlessness is not lingual

> ⁓

This is a thought the singing prompts in him.

> His feet are warmed by hot coals and soapstone
> he brought from home. He kneels in a box
> he built and paid for, within a box
> he built with his neighbors.
> The painted exterior came later,
> brought togetherness, but suffocates
> the cedar.
>
> ⁓

*the sea grew rough*

       *the well is deep*

              *no ghost has flesh and bones*      his lips open

      around syllables

              lets them out     around the world

breath

   by

      breath

        his utterance joins

    his shoulders rub to the breathing between

      those who are breathing

          together with the other mouths

where the group stops traveling is the distance to the ends

      of their breaths

individually or collectively   from each

      breath to each

        other breath    or from mouth

      to breath-end

**A bundle of wheat drawn delicately in the foreground**

**While everything else is solid and grieving**

Even at the close

Of day, there is another formation

On the base of the old

Day

A physician

Called after

Euphoria

In the kitchen the harvest evaporates

I sing pan

Tensile, lit,

body. any bounded aggregate of matter.

## Counting

I lived in the hovel beyond the wall. The stone
wall where I hovered. The wall was the edge
of my bower. The dog pulled things home. I gave
beds to those things I didn't bury:
teeth, birds, corpses and blinds.

*Press this moon-shape into me, hold*
*it there until the sunlight on my skin*

*uncovers its edge.* My dog reveals her teeth
when she is threatened but I bleach my teeth
to make them white as diamonds. I am

ten. Those four men admire me.
I am ten. Sparkling at the edge
of a stream, pond, swamp. Naked. I was then.

**The opposite of grass**


1.

"to lift, raise, heave"

I cannot lift it

Japan

2.

see, saw, swung

The moon is hung
Behind the woman with curlers in her hair

Her smock and the moon are white
People stand on the moving stairs
Jesus

The moon mocks the woman with curlers in her hair
She has only one breast
The back of her smock is the shade of the moon

3.

nine inches below

sea level, Oregon

rain coming down in combs

4.

and the lack of beds

was the thrashing temper of water

were the appetites of the rustic soldiers

*Paffuto*

5.

the question that cannot be asked without bending

6.

*ovaio,* [she is a]
"Good layer
(of eggs)"

## Vierge pour toujours dans le Petit Palais

I dashed from my arched room in which there was no perspective,

to my knees on the diamonds of the tile floor

harsh stage whispers of air currents warning me

so bright he was I could not see him

his light shone through my paleness and made a lamp of me

could I have said, Not me? could I have uttered any word?

giant bird harbinging the small white bird that entered me

I caught it in my mouth; its heart beat on my tongue

its feathers filled my mouth

I faltered


I'd wanted an ordinary baby
*bien triste*


    he smiles a tiny sickle, unwraps my breast
    I feed him milk
    I have not drunk

by the husband I am unknown
*Je ne l'ai jamais touché*

## Giacometti's Model

I thought he might open me, but he was the wrong artist: neurotic and baked in the fleshless 20th century. He chipped away at me in clay until I was feet and skull tenuously connected by a strand of rumpled bronze. He cast me outside the meaning of myself, making me dense and impenetrable. He drew me in loops and circles over and over my eyes my mouth until the paper wore away, and I felt him silencing and blinding me until all that counted were my prim shins, the chair, floor boards and walls. If he'd touched me once I would have opened my legs for him. If he'd touched me a thousand times I would have let him rearrange me the way he moved the cigarette pack and ashtray again and again as if his very life depended on their exact position on his nightstand.

At first I just wanted him to see me, but he saw me the same way he saw his mother— our portraits looked no different from one another— skeletal and stunned, charred corpses, his charcoal the dead fire that took our lives away. I wanted to blacken his eyes, scratch and smash his mouth as he did mine.

Day after day I sat on the hard chair in his attic under a bare bulb, like a criminal, only he was the thief. Too frozen to move or protest, knowing how he pared away my prickled flesh on the page made me colder still. The points of my pelvic bone ached. He made me thin, stole my female body's natural cushion. He wrung me out with his eyes, unjuiced me until he compressed my boundaries to within the narrow lines of the chair. Before I became too tired to feel, I felt like a child again, sitting upright and obedient, toeing the line between human and animal until I forgot how to cross it.

If the chair had been a plush settee, and he
Renoir...

I'd thought he might open me.

Why did he unclothe me only to
close me?

He never moved beyond the place

where art is a rebuff, a howl, a mirror.

I'd hoped we might at least lie down together once and make a double
imprint in the wet clay.

**Holding**

She experiments by picking the baby up, putting it down, picking it up again. She will turn off the lights for twelve hours, as a political act, which will also help the baby to sleep, she hopes. The cradle runs on batteries so that is her fallback position. When her arms tire.

Heavy equipment excavates her doorstep and shakes the curtains and dishes in her tiny rooms. She does not want to see the earth-smeared rocks turned up to the surface like naked slugs. The thought of them causes pressure in her chest, makes her try to draw too much air into her lungs. As she does, she visualizes the minute passages inside her baby's fragile lungs. Although they are probably soft and pink, she sees them as white and stiff like drinking straws.

The wallpaper is green with gray and white birds on delicate black branches. There are layers of other patterns underneath that she will never see, that have been seen by people who are old now or dead. She wants to have a house that is new, built just for her, whose walls she will be the first person to see. She would like this to happen before her baby is old enough to know the green wallpaper, but he is already beginning to respond to light and shape.

## He He He Palm Ash


whosoever apart, undo their dance, untwine atom from
molecule, no longer so small but pinging/ against/
concave sides of the cosmic pot
shining ring beyond which there is no
exterior
swallow, swallow it
whole
become
its casing

that the miniscule turn out to be
vast
and silver
silver minnow, singular
muscle upset the pond
upon which the pond
upends the bowl of itself

vexed

A baby with an aura, or was it
Halo, or was it only
Refraction
White faces bending
Toward him?

He is parked into the bottom corner
He is on a hard rock
He is on a purple blanket, he is on moist
Palm fronds he is on dried palm
Ash.

He is on the list of what I don't
Believe. He is light on the Atomic
Table

**Bastard of the emblem**

It was a casual adoption

Of the tree, Prunus Cerasus

Ending in an epithet of cheese

Ending in a scandalous bonk on the forehead

By a pit

A speckled boy who does not look dead

Flecked with mud

Sad because his horse has left him

Behind on the ground

Photographed as if upright,

Though he is supine

The boy whose lips possess as many curves

As lips can have and not be fleur-de-lis

Whose lips were prone to epithets,

Saliva

Whose chin is white and round

Mud all around

**byblow,**

misbegot, this or that word

(your beautiful drawing stolen and dropped in the road)

what mud cakes you?  same that makes my tongue


your steed is just a horse, love, but hay can be the walls of a house


a miracle blew your lost drawing of the Garden of Eden onto the steps of the rectory

(you became another scary or stupid story the nuns tell)

the silken back of a goat, a little boy with his coat flapped open like wings

## Icarus, dashed

In delirium flight
sinuous tired
hard
umbra
mist song I
with fathered wing
cliffed

arc'd
cartilage
stoned
days, days
aflame a-raw
umber limits

tips lashed
lashed to sky
lashed against
lashed to my burnt
cheekbone

stones slashed
salt tones

rush through my coiled
ear
*come home*

boiled
alone
heaven-
honed
light-
sheared

*HELD*

A whole host of simply performed but sonorous experiments between the surface and the drop leads to a second prayer inspired when the flood subsides.

He tips his rod. Waist-like indentations appear in a splashing, and ripples stall, unwilling to propagate over the surface of milk. How finely he tears.

A girl runs through puddles in her plastic raincoat that doesn't breathe and under which drops of sweat roll down her skin, trapped.

But drop does mingle with water, as I have not, in some heavy shower of rain, hoped to influence the condition of surface. On which floats a message, dinned with truth.

\

E is the electrical machine.
L is the light strip of iron held down.
D is the drop, resting

waiting to be made to splash. All this in the service of photographing the motion of the drop, so the nature of the motion of the drop is no longer conjecture. It is the conjugal relationship between the scientist and phenomenon: that he will wait for the drop, which is held in suspension, to fall; that he will go home tonight to his children, watch his wife pour warm milk into their glasses, kiss them.

**Love before casualty**

for getting the men to unarm    unname

      absence of fact:  remains

      distilled into boy, the minutes drop

dumplings into soup, drunkling, sop

can only watch: the barely women (k)new

      inside his skin

      jeweled under thin

        arms

        *

      by dead, lives dark

night bullied by moonlight, dust

      gums of earth

      birth broken stone,

a girl, jeweled, opens the mouth of world

      close and soon

## Position of apparent displacement

I have opened this rose into the space into which this rose opens

itself, wet, upon pockets of reflexivity where closure clenches its bite onto untamable oxygen. Air

pushes out the measured lengths of otherwise

visible fading and I am trying to assess the distance from where

the petal meets the front plane of the visual field and where my mind knows the flower

flows back to. The rose

curls into the curve of night. Beggars my space so I lie

under flat blankets, breathing. The spreading rose holds my breath

in chill when the sun and moon are together in the sky in early morning.

Remember the man who was a thin black slash on white snow seen from above. Benches boot-prints, a bird. The man is a branch and the thing falling from the branch. Onto the snow. A color would help.

A soldier makes snow angels, bringing gray into the black and white. She makes her wings with a gun, not arms. Now there is a woman and a man. Meaning is doubled. The abstraction of black lines and spots on the white snow doesn't answer the question. The man asks.

A woolen coat with quilted lining. Forgotten money, sewn into the lining. The coat is heavy in its weight and it tires you to wear it. Space between the fibers lets in the cold, so you are both tired and cold in the heavy coat. Your laboring breath blossoms into unlimnable vacancy.

A question is answered by blackness on snow. Who says the rose is red?

**Brahmakamal**


1.


How light it is above the dark rectangle. The composition is stolen.

> It isn't play, the light. Displayed in the shadow
> cast by the mountain, of the mountain
> that was paradise.

She watches what is still. She is the small obsidian window at which light scratches.


> The force of an armed man opens the gray space of lake, conjures sourceless light.


Eight or nine legs, each one named for a type of love. Children fragile as talc.


She is waiting out her papery night.


Fragrant, soundless.


2.

Children delicate as opiates.

Who flake apart like paper.

Gun-powder children.


Pressed on by opium, they steal away across the gray lake.

Water like paper.

Wet paper boats, dragging.

## Swell

The tide comes in and fills the house, ebbs and leaves us, shells

the children hold us to their ears, who never listen

tear themselves on us.

**Strong-Necked madonna**

Oh, girl in fleur-de-lis
pants Oh, man in belted robe

always the flower
        opens, sheer
and as a kind of slavery

        he touches her

with his bulbous sole
the long slow draft of holiness
        leaking against her
recoil

(C)love(n)

## Bleat and Sigh Night

Dear Gertrude,

I have tried to write you edemic letters and add juice to keep it plump.

The misusers torment the alphabet. A letter is an innocent. A letter is not an army.
The alphabet is weep. It is angry as in K. It is a chained ankle but it is not a shackle per
say. To say that it is a shackle is to say hatred is A.

For those who don't know, it is grace to process.

And this is why you should never rest: a ledger holds and shapes conflict.

As pages curl and limp you are subjected to a damaged aroma rising chimera-like as from
a steaming bowl of soup. Soup that is nurturing and a girl's locks fall into it at their tips.

Single stream recycling, what does it mean does it mean to crush a can under a foot a
green foil can can cut in a way similar to glass and if it is rusted will make you sick. Sick.

Up to your soft little egg-shaped eyes two of which can neither be in the center
of a head.

I want to remember this and I want honestly to be alone and softening almost to
liquid. I don't mind but do behave and my exile is complete and unrepentant.
One time and never again, a tone without echo. I am certain there are other sounds.

Shhhh. In this opening there is screaming and pieces of absence of light waiting
to be joined to a concept of darkness. Dark as pungency, fiber and acid, that makes your

eyes seep, in which is the seed of the small mistake that can be seen through. How round and red, how long and pink, how translucent and layered you are.

Dry sand, bare legs, monstrous stalking. Monstrous stalking and the gift of the absence of the monster. Never again the kindness of warmth. It was a kindness and a kind of meaning.

When the ceiling is torn away, years of dirt fall on your head. It is and it does. It is underground, which is not the end of the world but a question of slender ankles and sugar on your tongue when you are young. Moving in one direction makes life pleasant alright. It does. As long as there is polyphony under the line of your song.

Dear Gertrude, I want to, I badly want to. Does the bone protruding from my ear shock you? Character can change when a bone is thrown. An occasion is stirring so don't be surprised if there is nothing to eat. Cake is not nourishment but solace and solace is silence and statutes shake the mountain douse the tender. Darkness ignites training retraining shivering and more flammable drinking. Expiration stops a spark and on the whole binds us. River ringing the mountain is C.

There is little to sing but much to chop. Do not be sheepish. Eat the chop chiefly but do not chop the lamb. She is more than a little. Whisper, whisper against hearing.

**Glazed blind cushion not mercy**


Dear Gertrude,

On the side we were sleeping outside in the ache of evening and becoming mistook the chrysanthemum of dawn for resignation again and again between your thumb and fore-finger accepting no more numbness the ordinary fabric and hatred and particularity of the orbit.

Very well, my leg is uncertainly thinner than the rest and winter unending.

Pleased to not start singing again, this makes me sad.

We had no choice but to cook the cow, who cried in the meadow at her absurd fate. The resources of the plain are tangled with sickness, but memory is tender.

Sliced and served with cucumber. We have a languid meal and the red wine is better.

Consider the distinguishing palate, the peeling of onions for a reduction, not an occasion or education nor reparation for any outage, considering the way everything is education or occasion. How strangely the dog shows distress. Why is it restrained. Why is it cut.

In an altercation of pigeons, cuts are unkind. We are a kind of control. I forgot to mention the thinnest skin on top of everything, especially sound. Especially sound. We are unreasonable, unkind. Period.

Chase the wild goose. Baste with butter long and cool, pale and perfect dream, shatter the living tree and on the softening rotted wood, feast, dear unsober hope.

We pray that the region is not melting, and measuring is exaggerating. The sternum is the middle of our chest and is all that remains in the small space of praying.

What does it mean to comb? To divide a texture into miniscule parallel striations. My hair is in ribbons. The chicken wears a ribbon so it is a pet and will never be killed and cut into with the good knives. The room is all around us and kindness too but weakly. We eat and huddle darkly.

Aroma fails us. Eating is to like bullying.

We cannot get the rank civilians to leave, but it is a brave smell, it squats, it is a hot teakettle of duty, bearable and beginning again.

If you have a rump you know what to do with it. Sit it down and feel in your heart what sitting down is and the chair against you and your weight on the chair or in the chair we say in. Then you have no doubt what it is like to sit quietly. Noise is sound, happily. It cannot be inhaled and every day is the same day when the need for a drink is broken out into units. Which breaking makes a shattering sound.

Dear Gertrude, we are husbanded animals rolling around and around in the meadow until buffed. Then the meat is stringy and undesirable. But the mother is missing her young one and grief is one long uncleavable noise.

Yes, I suppose there is.

A monster in the house that was nothing and it is a certain kind of monster, how can I put this delicately, it has unstructured me and left my scaffolding in a clattering pile that cannot be denied as what was once not obvious but now lies exposed. Looking is eating and is not an oven. I like to eat dates.

Furniture is foolish and so is history and so is a hammer.

The man cut his foot on an old tin can and was carted away on a litter. Absorption is a thing in a way and it is a state. Take away the thing and why do you still have absorption. The state of him was cut, but he is not a woman. He is not a house.

Music is calming. It is simultaneous and temporal, but not simultaneity and not time.

Honestly.

Why not roast a galloping antelope? Keep it warm. There will be a lot of it. It sees you but is not seeking and doesn't find you beautiful.

I told the cow she could be anything. She considered me. You needn't be beef. You needn't be carved. She looked for me leaving her. I left her alone and forgot. The unreal smoothness of her hide, the dark, the moon, the hugeness, the falsehood of my pulse.

Hush night, Satin is asleep beneath the mountain. The mountain is a tool.

I am called turmeric, sunken, dashed, floating the drawn into me verdant lipsticked evidence of echo ringing your neck. I heard you digging, the chickens scratching around the pole. The chickens are blindfolded and alone. It is simple to save them but dinner is better and best of all is misbehavior, there is nothing sweeter. Nothing sweeter under the sky. A rain falls, rain drops, a wetting, a shift.

They are still alive which makes them soft and spongy under the knife. The softer the better. It is better there, under the napkin. The better there is meanness, the better taken away, the better don't think about it.

I remember bravely, my folded organ of recollection. Recital is the opposite of origami. How uneasily I unfold.

How easily medicine is balm and becoming and cloudy but never lonely.

There is no more yesterday, but let's pretend there is, and it is there.

The essence of vagueness is that it is violent and misleading and a mission and certainly political and it is also a fig. It is a violation claiming a way in. Claim is plated speech. Claim is a dead man hanging from a crane over the street. It is a movie. Please turn the sound down.

Dear Gertrude,

I imagine you at the oven. I see you tending your plants. Water pours from a spout like a wavering tongue thirsty for soil. You are saving. Heat scarred away by a sunlessness thin as a cold vinyl coat. See you next year the lilacs will smell as completely lilac as the past. We have primped, plumed, and exsanguinated, shrugged, ceded and sectioned. No matter how closely you listen you will hear nothing beneath applause. One is neither better than the other nor the end. Only superstition and being. Do not be unopening, there are reasons and there is logic. Stay and sleep. It is darkening and the sheep count.

Notes on the poems:

Italicized quotes in "Breath is a distance" were taken directly from *The New English Bible*, New York: Oxford University Press, 1972.

In the final stanza of "The opposite of grass", the definition was taken directly from *Cassell's Italian Dictionary*, New York: Macmillan, 1967.

"Vierge toujours dans le Petit Palais" was inspired by many paintings in the Petit Palais in Avignon, but primarily 15th century Annunciations by Bartolomeo della Gatta and Bartolomeo Caporali.

"The Architect's Sleep Is Flat and Deep," "and a wrinkle" and "The house is as clear as the panes in their steel frames" were seeded by the images in the book, *Houses,* by architects Kazuyo Sejima and Ryue Nishizawa/SANAA, published by ACTAR, Barcelona; and MUSAC, León; 2007.

"Glazed blind cushion not mercy" and "Bleat and Sigh Night", represent my attempt to know Gertrude Stein, as one poet to another, and one human being to another, via *Tender Buttons*. "Glazed blind cushion not mercy", corresponds to her section "Roast Beef" and "Bleat and Sigh Night" corresponds to "Mutton."

Thank you to the editors of the following publications where these poems appeared, sometimes in earlier versions.

*Arsenic Lobster*: "Saturated, darkening limbs claw the white sky";
*Caliban Online:* "Gate that Hunger Opened"; "Brahmakamal"; "Egress"; Strong-Necked Madonna"; "Bastard of the emblem"; "Glazed blind cushion not mercy"; "Bleat and Sigh Night";
*Court Green:* "September 13, 2008";
*Negative Capability Press* <u>*Thirty Three: An[niversary] Anthology*</u>*:* "Dear rowboat,";
the final stanza of "Glazed blind cushion not mercy" was posted on the *Poetry Pole*;
*Stonecoast Lines*: "Them"

I wish to express my gratitude to the following remarkable and cherished poets/friends: Gray Jacobik, for her profound generosity in sharing with me her formidable intellect, and whose trusted voice is always with me; Lissa Kiernan, without whom this book very possibly would not be, and most certainly wouldn't be this book: for her astute advice on ordering and for introducing my work to Negative Capability Press; Jeanne Marie Beaumont, for mentorship and support during and beyond Stonecoast; Kazim Ali for his mentorship at Stonecoast; Pamela St. Clair and Suzanne Levine, for intelligent, patient critiques and for preventing poetry from being a lonely pursuit; artists Gene Beery and Andrew Witkin for their alternative perceptions, kind receptivity and reciprocity; Rachel McMullen, editor at NCP, whose insights helped shape this manuscript.

I also want to acknowledge artisan A. Pepe, of Naples, Italy, who made the shepherd figurine on the cover. The Pepe family has been producing shepherds for crèches since 1478. I was fortunate to be able to consult Sophie Clarke for this information.

Most of all, I thank Chris Passehl, for his support: technical, aesthetic, and moral.

JANET PASSEHL maintains an active practice
in both visual art and poetry.
Her art has been exhibited and collected
in the U.S. and Europe, and she has
participated in cross-genre writing and visual
art projects in the U.K, notably Imagistic,
in Cardiff, Wales; and Translations, at the
University of Lincoln, Lincoln, England.
She received an MFA in Creative Writing/Poetry
from Stonecoast Writers program in 2010.
Her poems have been published
in Court Green, Arsenic Lobster,
and several issues of Caliban Online.
Clutching Lambs is her first poetry collection.
Janet lives in Essex, Connecticut, with her
husband Chris, their greyhound Lee Lee Belle,
and the ghosts of greyhounds past.

www.ingramcontent.com/pod-product-compliance
Lightning Source LLC
Chambersburg PA
CBHW062112090426

42741CB00016B/3398